AN ·

ORATION,

&c. &c.

Friends, Countrymen, and Fellow Citizens,

ON this day eighteen years a nation was born at once, a new order of things arose, and an illustrious æra in the history of human affairs commenced. The ties which before had joined us to Great Britain were severed, and we assumed a place among the nations of the earth.

Having delivered the first oration that was spoken in the United States, to celebrate this great event, I feel myself doubly honored in being again called upon, after a lapse of sixteen years, to perform the same duty. Were my abilities equal to the important subject, your entertainment would be great, but I must cast myself on your candor, and solicit indulgence, for falling far short of that display of eloquence which this eventful day is calculated to inspire.

It

It is worthy of remark, that the difcovery of America was nearly coincident with the invention of the art of printing, and of the mariner's compafs. From thefe three fources the condition of mankind has been greatly improved. By means of the art of printing, the darknefs of ignorance, which for many centuries had overfhadowed mankind, has given place to the light of knowledge, and learned men of every clime conftitute but one republic. In confequence of the mariner's compafs all the nations of our globe form one extended family, reciprocally adminiftering to the wants of each other. May I be allowed to add, that the difcovery of America was the firft link of a chain of caufes, which bids fair to enlarge the happinefs of mankind, by regenerating the principles of government in every quarter of the globe. Among the events refulting from this difcovery, and which led to that GREAT REVOLUTION, the declaration of independence, is confpicuoufly preeminent. I will not wound your ears, on this feftive day, by a repetition of the many injuries received by this country from Great Britain, which forced us to cut the gordian knot which before had joined us together. Suffice it to obferve, that for the twelve years preceding the 4th of July, 1776, claim rofe on claim, injury followed injury, and oppreffion trod on the heels of oppreffion, till we had no alternative left, but that of abject flavery or complete independence. The fpirit of freedom decided in favour of the latter: Heaven fmiled on our exertions. After an eight years war, in which our countrymen difplayed the patience, the perfeverance and the magnanimity of republicans, ftruggling for every

thing

An oration, delivered on the anniversary of American independence, July 4, 1794, in Saint Michael's Church, to the inhabitants of Charleston, South Carolina.

David Ramsey

AN
ORATION,

DELIVERED ON

THE ANNIVERSARY

OF

AMERICAN INDEPENDENCE,

JULY 4, 1794,

IN SAINT MICHAEL's CHURCH,

TO THE

INHABITANTS

OF

CHARLESTON, SOUTH CAROLINA,

BY DAVID RAMSEY, M. D.

PRESIDENT OF THE SENATE OF SOUTH CAROLINA.

" Oh, Liberty ! Heaven's choice Prerogative,
" True bond of Law, thou social Soul of Property,
" Thou Brea'h of Reason—for thee the valiant bled "

LONDON ·

Printed and Sold by Citizen DANIEL ISAAC EATON, Printer and
Bookseller to the Supreme Majesty of the People, at the COCK
AND SWINE, No. 74, Newgate-street.

1795.

PRICE FOUR PENCE.

thing that is dear to freemen, their most sanguine wishes were realized. The government of Great Britain, which began the war to inforce the claim, to bind us *in all cases whatsoever*, after spending a hundred millions of money, and sacrificing a hundred thousand subjects, to no purpose, was obliged to give up the contest, to retire from our shores, and to relinquish, by a solemn treaty, all claim to bind us *in any case whatsoever*. Such a triumph of liberty could not fail of vibrating round the world. A great and mighty nation on the other side of the Atlantic, in imitation of our example, has abolished a system of oppression, under which their forefathers for so many centuries had groaned. We trust and hope, that they will discover as great abilities in planning and executing a good NEW government as they have hitherto done in destroying an ancient bad one. Should this well-founded expectation be realized, we may hope that revolutions will follow revolutions, till despotism is banished from our globe. In this point of view, the enlarged philanthropist must not only rejoice in the benefits acquired by this country from its independence, but still more in those which are likely to flow from it to the oppressed of every country.

It may seem presumptuous for us, who are a nation of but yesterday, to arrogate to ourselves the merit of having enlightened mankind in the art of government: but we became an independent people under circumstances so favourable to the rights of man, that great indeed must have been our stupidity, had we not done so. When we review the origin of other nations, we find

A 3 that

that accidental circumstances had a principle share in forming their constitutions. At one time a successful invader, at another a daring chieftain, fixed the constituent parts of their government; but it never was known, anterior to our days, that a great, wise, and enlightened people, were peaceably convened by their representatives to deliberate on the principles of a constitution, by which they were to be governed. From the first settlement of this country, every thing concurred to inspire its inhabitants with the love of liberty: the facility of procuring landed property, gave every citizen an opportunity of becoming an independent freeholder. Remote from the influence of KINGS, BISHOPS, and NOBLES, the equality of rights was inculcated by the experience of every day. Having grown up to maturity under circumstances so favourable to liberty, and then being at once severed from all connection with the old world, the people of this country, in forming a constitution for their future government, had every incitement to establish such principles as promised to secure the greatest possible sum of political good, with the least possible portion of evil. When such a people became perfectly their own masters, and free to adopt any constitution they pleased, great would have been their shame had they not improved on those forms of government WHICH ORIGINATED IN TIMES OF DARKNESS, AND WERE INSTITUTED UNDER THE INFLUENCE OF PRIVILEGED ORDERS. On this anniversary of our independence it cannot be improper to shew, that this has actually been done, and that in consequence thereof we enjoy advantages, rights, and privileges, superior

perior to moſt, if not to all, of the human race. Bear with me, then, while I attempt to demonſtrate this, by a detail of particulars.

In entering on this ſubjeȼt, where ſhall I begin? Where ſhall I end? Proofs are unneceſſary, I need only appeal to experience. I have a witneſs in the breaſt of every one who hears me, and who knows the condition of the common people in other countries. In the United States the bleſſings of ſociety are enjoyed with the leaſt poſſible relinquiſhment of perſonal liberty. We have hit the happy medium between deſpotiſm and anarchy. Every citizen is perfeȼly free of the will of every other citizen, while all are equally ſubjeȼt to the laws. Among us no one can exercife any authority by virtue of birth. All ſtart equal in the race of life. No man is born a legiſlator. We are not bound by any laws but thoſe to which we have conſented. We are not called upon to pay our money to ſupport the idle-neſs and extravagance of court favourites. No bur-dens are impoſed on us, but ſuch as the public good re-quires. No enormous ſalaries are received by the few at the expence of the many. No taxes are levied but ſuch as are laid equally on the legiſlator and private ci-tizen. No man can be deprived of his life, liberty, or property, but by the operation of laws, freely, fairly, and by common conſent previously enaȼted.

The Liberty of the Preſs is enjoyed in theſe States, in a manner that is unknown in other countries. EACH CITIZEN THINKS WHAT HE PLEASES, AND SPEAKS

AND WRITES WHAT HE THINKS. Pardon me, illustrious Washington! that I have inwardly rejoiced
on seeing thy much respected name abused in our
newspapers. Slanders against thy adamantine charac-
ter, are as harmless as pointless arrows shot from
broken bows; but they prove, that our printing presses
are free. The doors of our legislative assemblies are
open, and the conduct of our state officers may be
safely questioned before the bar of the public, by any
private citizen. So great is the responsibility of men
in high stations among us, that it is the fashion to rule
well. We read of the rapacity, cruelty, and oppression
of men in power, but our rulers seem, for the most
part, to be exempt from these vices. Such are the
effects of governments formed on equal principles,
that men in authority cannot easily forget, that they
are the servants of the community over which they
preside. Our rulers, taken from the people, and at
stated periods returning to them, have the strongest incitement to make the public will their guide, and the
public good their end,

Among the privileges enjoyed by the citizens of these
States, we may reckon AN EXEMPTION FROM ECCLE-
SIASTICAL ESTABLISHMENTS. *These promote hypo-
crisy, and uniformly have been engines of oppression.*
They have transmitted error from one generation to
another, and restrained that free spirit of enquiry which
leads to improvement. In this country no priests can
decimate the fruits of our industry, nor is any prefer-
rence, whatever, given to one sect above another.

Religious

Religious freedom, banished from almost every other corner of the globe, has fixed her standard among us, and kindly invites the distressed from all quarters to repair hither. In some places fire and faggot await the man who presumes to exercise his reason in matters of faith. In others a national creed is established, and exclusion from office is inflicted on all, however worthy, who dare to dissent. In these happy States, it is a fundamental constitutional point, " that no religious " test shall ever be required as a qualification to any " office or public trust."

The experience of eighteen years has proved, that this universal equality is the most effectual method of preserving peace among contending sects. It has also demonstrated, that the church and state are distinct societies; can very well subsist without any alliance or dependence on each other. While the government, without partiality to any denomination, leaves all to stand on an equal footing, none can prove successful, but by the learning, virtue, and piety of its professors.

Our political situation, resulting from independence, tends to exalt and improve the minds of our citizens. GREAT OCCASIONS ALWAYS PRODUCE GREAT MEN. While we were *subjects*, the functions of government were performed *for* us, but not *by* us. To administer the public affairs of fifteen States, and of four millions of people, the military, civil, and political talents of many will be necessary. Every office, in each of these

multifarious

multifarious departments, is open to every citizen,
who has the abilities requisite for the difcharge of its
duties. Such prospects cannot fail of exciting a lau
dable ambition in our youth to make themselves worthy of public confidence.

It is one of the peculiar privileges we enjoy, in confequence of independence, that no individual, no
party-intereft, no foreign influence can plunge us into
war. Under our excellent conftitution, that fcourge of
nations will be avoided, unlefs unprovoked and unre-
dreffed injuries roufe the body of the people. Had we
not afferted our rank among nations, we, as appen-
dages to Great Britain, fhould this day have been engaged in hoftilities againft France, though bravely
ftruggling for the rights of man : and all this at the call
of a foreign mafter, and without any voice or will of
our own in the matter. Think of the cruel war now
carrying on by kings and nobles againft the equal
rights of man—call to mind the flaughtered thoufands,
whofe blood is daily fhedding on the plains of Europe,
and let your daily tribute of thanks afcend to the common Parent of the univerfe, who has eftablifhed you
in a feparate government, exempt from participating in
thefe horrid fcenes

To all the advantages of neutrality, we, as an independent people, are entitled by the laws of nations, of
nature, and of God. But it muft be acknowledged,
that at prefent we are deprived of many of them. The
fame fpirit which influenced Great Britain to attempt
the

the subversion of our independence, has led her to commit unwarranted outrages on our commerce. If the voice and interest of the people of that country was the rule of their government, as it is with us, those aggressions on our rights would never have taken place; but unfortunately for them, and for us, the interests of the great body of their subjects have been sacrificed to the fears and jealousies of their privileged orders. In the madness of their zeal to restrain France from doing what every independent nation has a right to do, they have needlessly plunged their own country into a ruinous war; and in the prosecution of it, instead of respecting our rights, as a neutral nation, they have treated us as if we were their subjects, bound to forego every branch of our accustomed, lawful commerce, that might, in their apprehension, contravene their designs. Many thanks to our worthy President, for his honest endeavors to preserve to us the blessings of peace. May they be successful. but if, on their failure, the last extremity must be resorted to, we may call heaven and earth to witness, that all the blood, and all the guilt of war, will lie at the door of Great Britain. Peace was our interest—peace was our wish; and for the preservation of it, the government and people of these States have done every thing that was reasonable and proper for them to do. May the sword of the United States never be unsheathed for the purposes of ambition. but if it must be uplifted in self-defence, may it fall with decisive effect on the disturbers of mankind. I beg pardon for this digression, and with pleasure turn away from contemplating the follies of that government, a

separation

separation from which we this day celebrate, that I may proceed in pointing out the superior advantages, which we, as an independent people, enjoy.

If we are to judge of the excellence of a government from its fruits, in the happiness of its subjects, we have abundant reason to be pleased with our own.—Since the peace of 1783, our country has been in a state of progressive improvement—debts, and other embarrassments, growing out of the late war, are, in most cases, nearly annihilated. Our numbers have been greatly augmented, both from the introduction of foreigners, and the natural increase of our own citizens. Our exports and imports have overflowed all their ancient boundaries. A revenue sufficient to support national credit, and to satisfy all other public exigencies, has been easily raised, and that without burdening the people. Upon an average, five of our CITIZENS do not pay as much to the support of government as one European SUBJECT. The whole sum expended in administering the public affairs of the United States, is not equal to the fourth part of what is annually spent in supporting one crowned head in Europe.

From the increase of our trade and population, new ports are daily opened, and new towns and cities *lift* their heads in all directions. The wilderness on our western frontier is constantly lessening by the extension of new settlements. Many who now hear me, have been witness to a legislature of a state, comfortably accommodated in a place, where seven years ago the trees of the

forest

forest had never experienced the axe of the husband-
man.

It was hoped by our enemies, and feared by our
friends, that the people of independent America would
not readily coalesce under a government sufficiently
energetic for the security of property and the preservation
of internal peace; but they have both been disappointed.
In these States, there is a vigorous exertion of the laws,
and an upright administration of justice. Property and
personal rights are well secured; criminals are easily
brought to suffer the punishment due to their demerits;
and no legal impediment exists in the way of creditors
recovering the full amount of what is due to them. These
blessings are secured to us without the intervention of a
standing army. Our government, resting on the affec-
tions of the people, needs no other support than that of
CITIZEN SOLDIERS. How unlike this to foreign countries, where enormous taxes are necessary to pay standing armies, and where standing armies are necessary to
secure the payment of enormous taxes.

Time would fail me to enumerate all the superior advantages our citizens enjoy under that free government
to which independence gave birth. I may observe,
in general, that as it proceeded from the people, it has
been administered for their benefit. The public good
has been the pole star by which its operations have been
directed.

That we may rightly prize our political condition, let
us

us cast our eyes over the inhabitants of the old world, and contrast their situation with our own.   A few among them are exalted to be more than men. but the great bulk of the people, bowed down under the galling yoke of oppression, are in a state of dependence which debases human nature.   In the benighted regions of Asia and Africa, ignorance and despotism frown over the unhappy land.   The lower classes are treated like beasts of burden, and transferred without ceremony from one master to another.   In some parts of Europe, the condition of the peasantry is not *quite so bad;* but in what country are the rights and happiness of the common people so much respected as in these States?   In this enumeration I purposely omit France.   Her former government was one of the worst.   We trust and hope, that when peace is restored, her enlightened rulers will furnish a new and strong proof of the connection between liberty and happiness.

Among the established governments of Europe, that of Great Britain deservedly stands high. what is faulty in that we have avoided, what is excellent in it we have transplanted in our own, with additions and improvements.   Is trial by jury the pride of Britons? It is in like manner the birth-right of our citizens.   Do Englishmen boast of the privileges they enjoy by virtue of the Act of Parliament, commonly called the Habeas Corpus Act?   We enjoy the same, and with more facility, for with us two magistrates (one of whom is of the quorum) are empowered to give all the relief to a confined citizen which is contemplated by that act.   Do

Englishmen

Englishmen glory in the Revolution of 1688, and of the cotemporary Acts of Parliament, which declared the rights and liberties of the subject? We have much more reason to be proud of our constitution. Whoever examines these declaratory acts of the English Parliament, will find, that all the provisions in favor of liberty which they contain, fly up and kick the beam, when weighed against the following single sentence of our constitution— " all power is originally vested in " the People, and all free governments are founded " on their authority, and instituted for their peace, " safety, and happiness."

It is true, that by the revolution of 1688, the people of England got a *foreign* prince to rule over them on better terms than their own *domestic tyrants* had done, but nevertheless, they only exchanged one master for another. for in their Act of Settlement, *to use their own words*, " they most humbly and faithfully submit- " ted themselves, their heirs, and their posterities " This æra was only the early dawn of that liberty, which shines on us in its noon-tide blaze. It was reserved for Americans to put government on its proper foundation, the sovereignty of the People.

Do Englishmen value themselves on what is called Magna Charta? In the preamble to this *celebrated* instrument, it is stated, that " the king, of his *mere free* " *will*, gave and granted to all freemen of his realm, the " liberties," which are therein specified. What is said to be thus given and granted by the free will of the sovereign,

vereign, we, the people of America, hold in our own
right. The sovereignty rests in ourselves, and instead of
receiving the privilege of free citizens as a boon from
the hands of our rulers, we defined their powers
by a constitution of our own framing, which prescribed
to them, that thus far they might go but no farther.
All power, not thus expressly delegated, is retained
Here let us pause, and leisurely survey the difference
between a CITIZEN and a SUBJECT. A free citizen,
of a free state, is the highest title of man. A subject is
born in a state of dependence, and bound to obey.
A citizen has within himself a portion of sovereignty,
and is capable of forming or amending the constitution,
by which he is to be governed; and of electing, or of
being elected, to the office of its first magistrate. In
monarchies, the subjects are what they are by the *grace
of their sovereign;* but in free representative governments, rulers are what they are by the GRACE of the
People.

In comparing the construction of the legislative assemblies of these states with the parliament of Great Britain, how striking the contrast! Here the representatives are appointed on such principles as collect and
transmit the real sentiments of the represented, but in
Great Britain the Parliament is a mockery of represen-
tation. The electors are but a handful of the whole
mass of subjects. Large towns have few or no representatives, while decayed boroughs are authorised to
send infinitely more than would be their quota on any
reasonable system. In these States, the legislative assemblies

femblies are like miniature pictures of the whole community, where each part retains its comparative impor-
tance, though on a reduced scale. In the parliament
of Great Britain, the few give law to the many. It has
been demonstrated, by calculations on this subject, that
the majority of the English house of commons is chosen
by less than eight thousand persons, though the kingdom
contains more than eight millions of subjects. Here the
views and wishes of the legislature are for the most part
the views and wishes of the people: but in England the
reverse is often the case. In the British Parliament, the
minister, with a penfioned majority, may carry what
schemes he pleafes; but in our legiflative affemblies,
every overture muft ftand or fall according to its real
or apparent tendency to help or hurt the people. Thus
might I go on, till I outraged your patience, in demon-
ftrating the fuperiority of our government over thofe
which are reputed the beft in the old world.

With fuch a conftitution, and with fuch extenfive territory, as we poffefs, to what height of national greatnefs
may we not afpire? Some of our large ftates have territory fuperior to the iflands of Great Britain, and the
whole together are little inferior to Europe itself. The
natural advantages of our country are many and great.
We are not left to depend on others for our fupport and
ftrength. Our luxurious foil is capable of producing,
not only enough for the increafing multitude that inha-
bits it, but a furplufage for exportation, fufficient to
fupply the wants of hundreds of thoufands in foreign
countries. Our numbers, if they continue to increafe as
B they

they hitherto have done, will, in lefs than a century, amount to forty millions. The light of fcience is kindling up in every corner of thefe States. Manufactures, and all the ufeful arts, are making a rapid progrefs among us, while agriculture, the firft and beft employment of man, furpafles all its ancient limits. With pleafure I could dwell on the pleafing profpect of our rifing greatnefs; but I haften to point out what is the line of conduct proper to be purfued by thofe who are fo highly favored. We ought, in the firft place, to be grateful to the all wife Difpofer of events, who has given us fo great a portion of political happinefs. To poflefs fuch a country, with the bleffings of liberty and peace, together with that fecurity of perfon and property, which refults from a well-ordered efficient government, is, or ought to be, matter of conftant thankfulnefs.

Induftry, frugality, and temperance, are virtues which we fhould eminently cultivate. Thefe are the only foundation on which a popular government can reft with fafety. Republicans fhould be plain in their apparel, their entertainments, their furniture, and their equipage. Idlenefs, extravagance, and diffipation of every kind, fhould be banifhed from our borders. It is from the induftrious alone that we can gather ftrength. The virtues now recommended are thofe which prepared infant Rome for all her greatnefs, and it is only from the practice of them that we can expect to attain that rank among nations, to which our growing numbers and extenfive territory entitle us to afpire.

While

While we celebrate this day, we should call to recollection those who have nobly fallen in support of independence. Time would fail to do them justice individually. To mention the names of some, seems a species of injury to others, who are equally deserving of our praise. It is the business of the historian to recite their names, and to tell their gallant deeds. Let us, while we recollect their virtues, be animated with the love of our country, that, like them, when called upon, we may die in its defence.

Many of those tried friends, who bravely fought our battles, or who wisely conducted our civil affairs through the late revolution, have taken their leave of this earthly stage, and a new generation has nearly grown up in their places. On them it depends to finish what their fathers have begun. Much is still wanting to perfect our internal police. As our government rests on the broad base of the People, every exertion should be made to diffuse virtue and knowledge among them. The *uninformed* and *misinformed* are fit tools to subserve the views of the turbulent and ambitious. Ignorance is the enemy of Liberty, and the nurse of Despotism. Let it therefore, be our study to multiply and facilitate the means of instruction, through every part of our country.

This would be a safe and constitutional antidote to aristocracy. In these States, where the rights of primogeniture are abolished—where offices are open to all—where elections are frequent, and the right of suffrage is universal and equal, if we go one step farther, and

give

give the poor the means of education, as well as the rich, our yeomanry can have nothing to fear from any man, or any affociation of men, however diftinguifhed by birth, office, fortune or abilities.

Had I a voice that could be heard from New Hampfhire to Georgia, ft fhould be exerted in urging the neceffity of diffeminating virtue and knowledge among our citizens. On this fubject, the policy of the eaftern ftates is well worthy of imitation. The wife people of that extremity of the Union, never form a new townfhip, without making arrangements that fecure to its inhabitants the inftruction of youth, and the public preaching of the gofpel. Hence their children are early taught to know their rights, and to refpect themfelves. They grow up good members of fociety, and ftaunch defenders of their country's caufe. No daring demagogue—no crafty Cataline—no ambitious Cæfar, can make any impreffion on the liberties of fuch an enlightened people.

To France is affigned the tafk of defending republicanifm by arms, but our duty is of a different kind. Separated by the wide Atlantic from the bloody diffentions of the old world, we fhould ftudy to cultivate every ufeful art—to enjoy in peace with all mankind the numerous bleffings which Providence has thrown in our way—to tranfmit them to pofterity, and to extend them to all within our reach. This ought to be the ambition of Americans, and not to feek an enlargement of their dominion, or to build their advancement on the degradation of others.

We

We should above all things, study to promote the union and harmony of the different States. Perish the man who wishes to divide us, into back country and low country, into a northen and southern, or into an eastern and western interest. Forming one empire we shall be truly respectable; but divided into two, or more, we must become the sport of foreign nations, and peace will be for ever exiled from our borders. The unity and indivisibility of the republic is an essential part of the French Constitution, so it ought to be with us. We should consider the people of this country, from the Mississippi to the Atlantic, from New Hampshire to Georgia, as forming one whole, the interest of which should be preferred to that of every part. Even the prejudices, peculiarities, and local habits of the different states, should be respected and tenderly dealt with.

The art of government has never been brought near to that degree of perfection of which it is capable. It is lamentably true that it seldom or never has been administered with any express view to its proper object, the happiness of the governed. We should be fired with the generous ambition of teaching mankind, by our example, that the people are capable of governing themselves to better purpose than it ever has been done by *kings* and *privileged orders*. Men of high rank, in Europe, have asserted, that a government formed at noon, on the equal principles we have adopted, would terminate before the setting of the sun. This day begins the nineteenth year of ours, and it is now stronger, and more firmly established than it ever was. We know by

experience

experience, that the coftly pageantry of kings and courts, is not effential to political happinefs   From the vigour of our free government, and effentially from its anfwering every purpofe that a government ought to anfwer, the world may learn, that there is no neceffity, in the nature of things, for man to lord it over man.   Inferences may be fairly drawn from our prefent happy political fituation, which lead to the extirpation of defpotifm from the face of the globe.   Let us forward this defirable revolution, not by officioufly intermeddling with the internal polity of foreign countries, but by exhibiting fuch an accumulation of private virtue and public happinefs, that other nations, ftuck with the fruits of our excellent conftitution, may be induced, from free choice, to new model their own on fimilar principles.

The eyes of the world are fixed on this country and on France.   The abettors of tyranny are anxioufly looking for opportunities to difcredit the new doctrines of the Rights of Man.   They on every occafion, reprefent them as leading to confufion and anarchy   Equality of rights, and equality of property, is, in their opinion, one and the fame thing.   Let the wifdom of our laws, and the orderly conduct of our citizens, difappoint their wifhes, and give the lie to their calumnies. Let us teach them, by our example, that genuine republicanifm is friendly to order, and a proper fubordination in fociety—that it is hoftile to mobs, and licentioufnefs of every kind, but the firm fupporter of conftituted

ftituted authorities—the guardian of property, as well as of the rights of man.

France is daily proving, that a handful of citizens, fighting under the banners of Liberty, is more than a match for an hoft of mercenaries, engaged in fupport of Tyranny. It remains for us to recommend free governments, by the example of a peaceable, orderly, virtuous, and happy people. We fhould prefs forward in accomplifhing every thing that can add to the common ftock of public good While war, with its horrid attendants, is the paftime of kings, let it be the ftudy of republicans, to make unceafing advances in every thing that can improve, refine or embellifh fociety. Animated with this noble ambition, the fuperior happinefs of our country will amply repay us for the blood and treafure which independence has coft. May that ambition fire our breafts, and may that happinefs increafe, and know no end, till time fhall be no more.

FINIS.

CPSIA information can be obtained
at www.ICGtesting.com
Printed in the USA
BVHW011547050521
606573BV00006B/276

The Essential Crockpot Cookbook

Super-Easy Recipes for Busy
People on a Budget

Betty Kern

TABLE OF CONTENTS

INTRODUCTION

The Mediterranean diet has become popular for its emphasis on healthy eating: fruits, vegetables, whole grains, fish and nuts. The Mediterranean diet has long been popular in the region where it originated; however, it has recently become popular in the United States and other nations. Researchers have also found strong evidence that the Mediterranean diet may reduce the risk for a number of medical conditions.

Today's busy world makes it hard to eat well and still be on time to work. In this book, I share recipes that take only 15 minutes to prepare so you can prepare everything in advance. I also share healthy fast food alternatives you can easily make on your way home from work or school. These recipes will make your week easier and more enjoyable so you can spend more time with your family and friends and less time in a restaurant or fast-food joint.

The Mediterranean diet has long been popular in the region where it originated; however, it has recently become popular in the United States and other nations. Researchers have also found strong evidence that the Mediterranean diet may reduce the risk for a number of medical conditions. This cookbook is designed to help you put this diet into practice for yourself as well as your family members and friends. I provide both vegetarian and meat-based recipes that are easy to prepare on weekdays or at weekends when you have more time. The recipes are divided into several weekly segments, so you can cook them all at once or pick and choose which ones you want to make each week.

The Mediterranean Diet, which is high in whole grains, fruits, vegetables, and olive oil, is linked to a lower risk of coronary heart disease. It also helps to keep your blood sugar and cholesterol levels in check.

In addition to watching what you eat, you also need to cook food. Eating healthy doesn't mean that you have to spend hours slaving in the kitchen. The Mediterranean Diet Crock pot Cookbook is packed with easy recipes that take just minutes to prepare.

The recipes in this book are geared toward busy people on a budget who still want to eat healthy. So whether you're vegetarian, vegan, or a meat-eater, all of the meals can be easily prepared at home. These hearty, exotic dishes will make you feel like you're enjoying the best meal ever!

You don't have to be a chef to enjoy authentic Mediterranean cuisine in the comfort of your own home. Mediterranean Diet Crockpot Cookbook for Beginners has designed this cookbook to help you make delicious, healthy meals in a fraction of the time it takes to cook in a restaurant.

Inside, you'll find more than 50 recipes that can be prepared with the click of a button. All of our recipes are healthy and easy to make. Plus, each recipe includes a detailed prep and cooking guide that leads you step-by-step through the preparation process.

You'll also find several handy accessories in this cookbook that you can use to prepare even more delicious recipes. We've included an assortment of food items, cutlery, and equipment that will help you prepare a wide variety of meals at home.

We encourage you to take advantage of all the great recipes included in this cookbook. We're confident that you'll be able to prepare delicious, healthy meals on a budget.

POULTRY RECIPES

1. Tender Onion Turkey Mix

Preparation time: 10 minutes

Cooking time: 7 hours

Servings: 4

INGREDIENTS:

- 1-pound turkey breast, skinless, boneless, and cubed
- 1 teaspoon turmeric powder
- ½ teaspoon garam masala
- ½ cup coconut cream
- 1 red onion, chopped
- ½ cup chicken stock
- 4 garlic cloves, minced
- ¼ cup chives, chopped

DIRECTIONS:

1. In your crock pot, mix the turkey with turmeric, garam masala, and the other ingredients except for the coconut cream, toss, put the lid on, and cook on Low for 6 hours.
2. Add the coconut cream, toss, put the lid on again, cook on Low for 1 more hour, divide everything between plates and serve.

NUTRITION: 206 calories, 20.8g protein, 10.6g carbohydrates, 9.2g fat, 2.1g fiber, 49mg cholesterol, 1253mg sodium, 498mg potassium.

2. Poultry and Apples Mix

Preparation time: 10 minutes

Cooking time: 7 hours

Servings: 4

INGREDIENTS:

- 1-pound chicken breast, skinless, boneless, and sliced
- 1 cup apples, cored and cubed
- 1 teaspoon olive oil
- 1 red onion, sliced
- 1 tablespoon oregano, chopped
- ½ teaspoon turmeric powder
- ½ teaspoon chili powder
- 1 cup chicken stock
- 1 tablespoon chives, chopped

DIRECTIONS:

1. Grease the crock pot with the oil, and mix the chicken with the apples, onion, and the other ingredients inside.
2. Toss, put the lid on, cook on Low for 7 hours, divide the mix between plates and serve.

NUTRITION: 187 calories,24.9g protein, 11.6g carbohydrates, 4.5g fat, 2.6g fiber, 73mg cholesterol, 254mg sodium, 558mg potassium.

3. Chicken with Oregano

Preparation time: 5 minutes

Cooking time: 7 hours

Servings: 4

INGREDIENTS:

- 1-pound chicken breasts, skinless, boneless, and sliced
- 4 scallions, chopped
- 2 endives, shredded
- ½ cup tomatoes, cubed
- 1 cup chicken stock
- 1 tablespoon oregano, chopped

DIRECTIONS:

1. In your crock pot, combine the chicken slices with the scallions and the other ingredients except for the endives and the oregano, toss, put the lid on and cook on Low for 6 hours.
2. Add the remaining ingredients, cook on Low for 1 more hour, divide everything between plates, and serve.

NUTRITION: 274 calories,36.8g protein, 11.5g carbohydrates, 9.3g fat, 9.1g fiber, 101mg cholesterol,3496mg sodium, 1198mg potassium.

4. Basil Chicken

Preparation time: 5 minutes

Cooking time: 5 hours

Servings: 4

INGREDIENTS:

- 1-pound chicken wings halved
- 1 tablespoon olive oil
- 1 tablespoon honey
- 1 cup chicken stock
- 1 tablespoon basil, chopped
- ½ teaspoon cumin, ground

DIRECTIONS:

1. In your crock pot, mix the chicken wings with the oil, honey, and the other ingredients, toss, put the lid on and cook on High for 5 hours.
2. Divide the mix between plates and serve with a side salad.

NUTRITION: 417 calories, 22.8g protein, 17.1g carbohydrates, 28.4g fat, 0.4g fiber, 90mg cholesterol, 554mg sodium, 169mg potassium.

5. Chicken and Broccoli Mix

Preparation time: 10 minutes

Cooking time: 5 hours

Servings: 4

INGREDIENTS:

- 1-pound chicken breast, skinless, boneless, and sliced
- 1 cup broccoli florets
- ½ cup tomato sauce
- ½ cup chicken stock
- 1 tablespoon avocado oil
- 1 yellow onion, sliced
- 3 garlic cloves, minced
- 1 tablespoon cilantro, chopped

DIRECTIONS:

1. In your crock pot, mix the chicken with the broccoli, tomato sauce, and the other ingredients, toss, put the lid on and cook on High for 5 hours.
2. Divide the mix between plates and serve hot.

NUTRITION: 165 calories, 25.7g protein, 6.8g carbohydrates, 3.5g fat, 1.9g fiber, 73mg cholesterol, 323mg sodium, 656mg potassium.

6. Cumin Chicken

Preparation time: 10 minutes

Cooking time: 7 hours

Servings: 4

INGREDIENTS:

- 1-pound chicken thighs, boneless, skinless, and sliced
- 1 tablespoon avocado oil
- 1 teaspoon cumin, ground
- 1 tablespoon rosemary, chopped
- 1 cup chicken stock
- 1 tablespoon chives, chopped

DIRECTIONS:

1. In your crock pot, mix the chicken with the oil, cumin, and the other ingredients, toss, put the lid on and cook on Low for 7 hours.
2. Divide the mix between plates and serve.

NUTRITION: 228 calories,33.2g protein, 1.2g carbohydrates, 9.2g fat, 0.6g fiber, 101mg cholesterol, 290mg sodium, 310mg potassium.

7. Whole Chicken Roast

Preparation Time: 10 minutes

Cooking Time: 4 hours and 10 minutes

Servings: 4

INGREDIENTS

- 2 Tbs of chicken fat
- 2 Tbs of granulated stevia sweetener
- 1 Tbs of chili powder
- 1 Tbs of smoked paprika
- 2 tsp of fresh basil finely chopped
- 1 tsp of fresh thyme finely chopped
- 1 of bone broth or water
- 1/2 cup of red wine
- 1 whole chicken, rinsed and dried
- Salt and freshly ground black pepper to taste

DIRECTIONS:

1. In a bowl, combine stevia sweetener, chili powder, smoked paprika, basil, and thyme.
2. Grease generously your Crock pot with the chicken fat.
3. Season the chicken with the salt and pepper, and rub well with the chili mixture.
4. Place the chicken in your Crock pot and pour with broth and wine.
5. Cover the lid and cook on HIGH for 3 to 4 hours.
6. Let the chicken rests for 10 minutes and serve.

NUTRITION: Calories: 599 Saturated Fat: 3g Trans Fat: 0g Carbohydrates: 91g Fiber: 22g Sodium: 534mg Protein: 35g

8. Slow Cooked Marinated Turkey Breast

Preparation Time: 5 minutes

Cooking Time: 6 hours and 5 minutes

Servings: 4

INGREDIENTS

- 1 lemon juice
- ¼ cup of olive oil
- 4 cloves of garlic minced
- 2 to 3 Tbs of fresh rosemary finely chopped
- 2 Tbs of fresh parsley chopped
- Salt and ground pepper to taste
- 2 turkey fillets (about 1 1/2 lbs)

DIRECTIONS:

1. In a bowl squeeze lemon juice, and combine with olive oil, and the spices.
2. Place turkey in a marinade, and refrigerate for 3 hours.
3. Place marinated turkey meat in a Crock pot with marinade.
4. Cover the lid and cook on LOW for 5-6 hours.
5. Serve.

NUTRITION: Calories: 599 Saturated Fat: 3g Trans Fat: 0g Carbohydrates: 91g Fiber: 22g Sodium: 534mg Protein: 35g

9. Cheesed Chicken Patties

Preparation Time: 15 minutes

Cooking Time: 5 hours and 15 minutes

Servings: 4

INGREDIENTS

1. 1 lb of minced chicken breast
2. 1 large egg
3. 1/4 cup of almond flour
4. 1 Tbs of fresh oregano finely chopped
5. 3 Tbs of olive oil
6. Salt and ground black pepper
7. 1/4 tsp of spicy paprika
8. 1/4 tsp of turmeric
9. 1/3 lb of hard table cheese (Cheddar or Parmesan)
10. Instructions
11. In a large bowl, add the minced chicken and all remaining ingredients.
12. Knead until all ingredients combined well; refrigerate for at least 30 minutes.
13. From the mixture shape patties, and top each with a slice of cheese.
14. Grease with the oil or chicken fat the bottom of your Crock pot.
15. Add stuffed patties and pour little water.
16. Cover the lid and cook on LOW for 4 to 5 hours.
17. Serve hot.

NUTRITION: Calories: 599 Saturated Fat: 3g Trans Fat: 0g Carbohydrates: 91g Fiber: 22g Sodium: 534mg Protein: 35g

10. Ale - Chicken and Zucchini "Meatballs"

Preparation Time: 15 minutes

Cooking Time: 5 hours and 15 minutes

Servings: 4

INGREDIENTS

- 2 Tbsp of chicken fat softened
- 1 1/2 lbs of ground chicken meat
- 2 zucchini grated
- 2 spring onions finely chopped
- 2 cloves of garlic
- 2 to 3 Tbs of fresh chopped parsley
- 1 large egg
- 1/2 cup of almond flour or ground almonds
- 1 tsp of cumin
- 1 tsp of ground paprika
- salt and ground black pepper to taste
- 3/4 cup of light beer

DIRECTIONS:

1. In a large bowl, add all ingredients except for beer and water.
2. Knead until all ingredients combined well.
3. Place the bowl in the refrigerator for 1 hour.
4. Add the chicken fat in the bottom of your Crock pot.
5. From the mixture shape balls and place in Crock pot.
6. Pour the beer over chicken meatballs.
7. Cover the lid and cook on LOW for 4 to 5 hours.

8. Serve hot.

NUTRITION: Calories: 599 Saturated Fat: 3g Trans Fat: 0g
Carbohydrates: 91g Fiber: 22g Sodium: 534mg Protein: 35g

11. Chicken Breast with Red Wine

Preparation Time: 35 minutes

Cooking Time: 3 hours and 35 minutes

Servings: 4

INGREDIENTS

- 2 Tbsp of chicken fat, melted
- 1 1/4 lbs chicken breasts - boned and skinned
- salt and ground black pepper to taste
- 2 crushed garlic cloves
- 1 1/4 of cups red wine
- 1 1/4 cups bone broth (preferably homemade) or water

DIRECTIONS:

1. Grease your Crock pot generously with the chicken fat.
2. Season the chicken breast with the salt and pepper.
3. Chop up the garlic and rub it into chicken breast and place in greased Crock pot.
4. Pour the bone broth (or water) and red wine and cover.
5. Cook on LOW for 3 to 3 1/2 hours or until the chicken reaches 165F on the inserted thermometer.

NUTRITION: Calories: 599 Saturated Fat: 3g Trans Fat: 0g Carbohydrates: 91g Fiber: 22g Sodium: 534mg Protein: 35g

12. Chicken Meatballs with Cheese Sauce

Preparation Time: 10 minutes

Cooking Times: 30 minutes

Servings: 4

INGREDIENTS

- 2 lbs minced chicken
- 1 large egg preferably organic
- 2 Tbs ground almonds
- Tbs grated Parmesan cheese
- Salt and black pepper to taste
- 1/2 cup olive oil
- For cheese sauce
- 1 3/4 cups of almond milk
- 4 1/2 oz Cheddar cheese
- 1 Tbs fresh parsley finely chopped
- Salt and white ground pepper to taste

DIRECTIONS:

1. Combine all ingredients for the meatballs in a shallow bowl.
2. Knead well until getting a homogeneous mixture.
3. From the mixture make the meatballs.
4. Heat the oil in a large frying skillet until shimmering.
5. Cook, until browned on all sides or about 10 to 12 minutes.
6. Place them on a platter with absorbent paper to drain.
7. Pour the milk in a saucepan and bring to boil.

8. Meanwhile, cut the cheese into pieces and add it to the milk stirring continuously until melt.

9. Finally, add salt, pepper and parsley; stir well.

10. Pour the sauce over meatballs.

11. Serve and enjoy!

NUTRITION: Calories: 599 Saturated Fat: 3g Trans Fat: 0g Carbohydrates: 91g Fiber: 22g Sodium: 534mg Protein: 35g

13. Chicken with Cabbage Stew

Preparation Time: 30 minutes

Cooking Time: 8 hours

Servings: 4

INGREDIENTS

- 2 lb chicken breast boneless skinless
- 4 cups cabbage, chopped (common and red)
- 1 small carrot sliced
- 1/2 cup green onions chopped (only green parts)
- 2 cups of water
- 1/4 tsp fresh thyme finely chopped
- 1/4 tsp fresh tarragon finely chopped
- 1/4 tsp nutmeg ground
- 1/8 tsp ground paprika
- 2 Tbsp olive oil
- Salt and pepper to taste

DIRECTIONS:

1. Rinse the cabbage and remove the loose outermost leaves so only clean, compact leaves remain.
2. Cut the very bottom of the stem.
3. Slice the cabbage, and then finely chop.
4. Cut the chicken breast in cubes.
5. Place all ingredients in your Crock pot.
6. Stir until combined well.
7. Cover the lid and cook on LOW setting 6 - 8 hours.
8. Taste and adjust seasonings to taste.
9. Serve hot.

NUTRITION: Calories: 599 Saturated Fat: 3g Trans Fat: 0g Carbohydrates: 91g Fiber: 22g Sodium: 534mg Protein: 35g

14. Chicken Breast with Creamy Broccoli

Preparation Time: 30 minutes

Cooking Time: 4 hours

Servings: 4

INGREDIENTS

- 2 Tbs of fresh butter melted
- 1/2 lb of chicken breast boneless, cut into cubes
- 1 lb of fresh broccoli
- 2 carrots sliced
- 1 cup of cooking cream
- 1/2 cup of grated cheese
- salt and ground white pepper to taste

DIRECTIONS:

1. Add melted butter in your Crock pot.
2. Season the chicken, and add in a Crock pot.
3. Add the broccoli flowerets, carrots, cooking cream and grated cheese; toss to combine.
4. Cover and cook on LOW for 3 to 4 hours.
5. Serve hot.

NUTRITION: Calories: 599 Saturated Fat: 3g Trans Fat: 0g Carbohydrates: 91g Fiber: 22g Sodium: 534mg Protein: 35g

15. Classic Tuscan Chicken Thighs

Preparation Time: 5 minutes

Cooking Time: 6 hours and 5 minutes

Servings: 4

INGREDIENTS

- 2 Tbs of chicken fat melted
- 1 red bell pepper, sliced
- 1/2 cup of grated Parmesan cheese
- 1/2 cup of heavy cream
- 1/2 cup of water
- 2 bay leaves
- 1 tsp of dried oregano
- 1/2 tsp of onion powder
- 1 tsp of garlic powder
- 2 lb bone-in chicken thighs
- Salt and freshly ground black pepper to taste

DIRECTIONS:

1. Add melted chicken fat, sliced bell pepper, Parmesan, heavy cream, water and herbs in your Crock pot and stir well.
2. Season the chicken generously with the salt and pepper and add into Crock pot: toss to combine well.
3. Cook on LOW heat for 6 to 8 hours or on HIGH heat for 4 hours.
4. Serve hot with extra Parmesan cheese.

NUTRITION: Calories: 599 Saturated Fat: 3g Trans Fat: 0g Carbohydrates: 91g Fiber: 22g Sodium: 534mg Protein: 35g

16. Creamy Meatballs with Mushrooms

Servings: 6

Preparation Time: 6 hours and 15 minutes

INGREDIENTS

- Meatballs
- 1 lb of minced beef
- 1 onion finely chopped
- 1 clove of garlic finely grated
- 1/2 bunch of parsley finely chopped
- 1 tsp of salt and ground black pepper
- 1 Tbs of water
- 1/4 cup of olive oil
- Mushrooms
- 3/4 lb of fresh or canned mushrooms
- 2 Tbs of olive oil
- 1 tsp of fresh butter melted
- 1 Tbs of minced garlic
- salt and ground black pepper
- 1/2 tsp turmeric
- 1 cup of cooking cream

DIRECTIONS:

1. In a large bowl, combine all ingredients for meatballs and knead well.
2. Cover and refrigerate for 1 hours.
3. Make the meatballs from mixture, and place in your greased Crock pot.

4. Combine all ingredients for Mushrooms and pour over the meatballs.
5. Cover and cook on LOW for 6 hours.
6. Taste and adjust seasonings.
7. Serve hot.

NUTRITION: Calories: 599 Saturated Fat: 3g Trans Fat: 0g Carbohydrates: 91g Fiber: 22g Sodium: 534mg Protein: 35g

PORK RECIPES

17. Mediterranean Pork Tenderloin

Preparation Time: 10 minutes

Cooking Time: 2 hours

Servings: 4

INGREDIENTS:

- 4 cloves garlic, crushed and minced
- 1 cup chicken broth
- 1 tablespoon garam masala
- Salt and pepper to taste
- 16 oz. pork tenderloin, trimmed
- 1 cup couscous
- ½ cup raisins
- ½ cup almonds, sliced and toasted
- 2 tablespoons red wine vinegar
- ½ cup fresh parsley, minced
- ½ cup olive oil

DIRECTIONS:

1. Add the garlic and broth to the crock pot.
2. In a bowl, mix the garam masala, salt and pepper.
3. Rub this mixture on both sides of the pork.
4. Add the pork to the crock pot.
5. Cover the pot.
6. Cook on low for 2 hours.
7. Transfer the pork to a cutting board.

8. Let rest for 2 minutes before slicing.

9. Skim the fat off the cooking liquid in the pot.

10. Add the raisins and couscous and cook on high for 15 minutes.

11. Add the almonds and mix well.

12. In another bowl, combine the vinegar, oil and parsley.

13. Serve the pork with the couscous and vinaigrette.

NUTRITION: Calories 682 Total Fat 35.9g Saturated Fat 5.6g Cholesterol 83mg Sodium 270mg Total Carbohydrate 52.2g Dietary Fiber 4.6g Total Sugars 11.5g Protein 39.9g Potassium 883mg

18. Mediterranean Pork Roast

Preparation Time: 15 minutes

Cooking Time: 6 hours

Servings: 8

INGREDIENTS:

- 4 teaspoons Greek seasoning, divided
- 1 pork loin roast (boneless), fat trimmed
- 2 fennel bulbs, sliced
- 4 tomatoes, chopped
- ½ cup reduced-sodium chicken broth
- 2 tablespoons reduced-sodium chicken broth
- Salt and pepper to taste
- 2 teaspoons cornstarch
- 1 ½ teaspoons Worcestershire sauce
- ¼ cup black olives, chopped

DIRECTIONS:

1. Sprinkle 1 teaspoon Greek seasoning on both sides of the pork.
2. Add the fennel to the crock pot.
3. Put the pork on top.
4. Add the tomatoes around the pork.
5. Pour ½ cup chicken broth to the crock pot.
6. Stir in the salt, pepper and remaining Greek seasoning.
7. Cover the pot.
8. Set it to low and cook for 6 hours.
9. Stir the remaining broth with the cornstarch and Worcestershire sauce.

10. Pour the sauce over the pork and sprinkle with olives on top before serving.

NUTRITION: Calories 213 Total Fat 8.6g Saturated Fat 2.9g Cholesterol 66mg Sodium 254mg Total Carbohydrate 8.5g Dietary Fiber 2.7g Total Sugars 1.9g Protein 24.9g Potassium 755mg

19. **Pork Chops & Couscous**

Preparation Time: 10 minutes

Cooking Time: 8 hours

Servings: 6

INGREDIENTS:

- ¾ cup low-sodium chicken broth
- 2 tablespoons olive oil
- 2 ¼ teaspoons dried sage
- 1 teaspoon oregano
- 1 teaspoon basil
- ½ tablespoon garlic powder
- ½ tablespoon paprika
- ¼ teaspoon dried thyme
- ¼ teaspoon dried marjoram
- ¼ teaspoon dried rosemary
- 2 lb. pork chops, fat trimmed (boneless)
- 2 cups couscous, cooked

DIRECTIONS:

1. Combine the chicken broth, olive oil and spices in a bowl.
2. Make slits on the pork chops.
3. Pour the spice mixture into your crock pot.
4. Add the pork and turn to coat evenly.
5. Seal the pot.
6. Cook on low for 8 hours.
7. Serve pork chops with couscous.

NUTRITION: Calories 561 Total Fat 32.1g Saturated Fat 11.1g Cholesterol 98mg Sodium 91mg Total Carbohydrate 34.5g Dietary Fiber 2.6g Total Sugars 0.2g Protein 31.4g Potassium 484mg

20. Creamy Pork Chops with Potatoes

Preparation Time: 10 minutes

Cooking Time: 4 hours

Servings: 4

INGREDIENTS:

- Cooking spray
- 4 pork chops
- 6 potatoes, cubed
- 1 cup milk
- 1 packet dry ranch dressing mix
- Garlic salt and pepper to taste
- 3 cups cream of onion soup

DIRECTIONS:

1. Coat a crock pot with oil.
2. Arrange the potatoes inside the pot.
3. Top with the pork chops.
4. Mix the rest of the ingredients in a bowl.
5. Pour this mixture over the pork chops and potatoes.
6. Seal the pot.
7. Set it to high and cook for 4 hours.
8. Pour the sauce over the pork chops and potatoes before serving.

NUTRITION: Calories 488 Total Fat 11 g Saturated Fat 4 g Cholesterol 95 mg Sodium 674 mg Potassium 2034 mg Total Carbohydrate 57 g Dietary Fiber 5 g Protein 36 g Total Sugars 7 g

21. Mediterranean Pork Chops

Preparation Time: 15 minutes

Cooking Time: 6 hours

Servings: 6

INGREDIENTS:

- 6 pork chops
- Garlic salt and pepper to taste
- 2 teaspoons dried basil
- 1 teaspoon oregano
- 2 teaspoons paprika
- 3 tablespoons olive oil
- 4 tablespoons balsamic vinegar
- 8 oz. chicken broth
- 1 cup carrot, cubed
- 1 cups potato, cubed

DIRECTIONS:

1. Coat the crock pot with cooking spray.
2. Sprinkle both sides of the pork chops with garlic salt, pepper, basil, oregano and paprika.
3. Transfer to the crock pot.
4. Mix the balsamic vinegar and olive oil.
5. Pour into the pot.
6. Pour in the chicken broth.
7. Stir in the carrots and potatoes.
8. Cover your pot.
9. Cook on low for 6 hours.

NUTRITION: Calories 344 Total Fat 27.2g Saturated Fat 8.5g Cholesterol 69mg Sodium 190mg Total Carbohydrate 4.8g Dietary Fiber 1.1g Total Sugars 1.2g Protein 19.3g Potassium 448mg

22. Pork with Sweet Potatoes & Mushrooms

Preparation Time: 15 minutes

Cooking Time: 5 hours

Servings: 2

INGREDIENTS:

- 1 lb. pork tenderloin, diced
- 1 yellow bell pepper, sliced
- 1 zucchini, sliced into rounds
- 1 sweet potato, cubed
- 1 tablespoon olive oil
- 2 onions, sliced
- 1 clove garlic, minced
- ¼ cup tomato sauce
- 2 cups pork broth
- 1 teaspoon dried oregano
- Pepper to taste
- 1 cup mushrooms

DIRECTIONS:

1. Put the pork, bell pepper, zucchini and sweet potato into the crock pot.
2. In a pan over medium heat, add the oil and cook the onion for 2 minutes.
3. Stir in the garlic and cook for 2 minutes.
4. Transfer the onion and garlic to the crock pot.
5. In the same pan, pour in the tomato sauce and broth.
6. Season with the pepper and oregano.

7. Boil and then transfer to the crock pot.
8. Mix everything.
9. Cover the pot and cook on low for 3 hours.
10. Stir in the mushrooms and cook on low for another 1 hour.

NUTRITION: Calories 572 Total Fat 17.1g Saturated Fat 4.2g Cholesterol 166mg Sodium 1092mg Total Carbohydrate 34.6g Dietary Fiber 7.3g Total Sugars 15.7g Protein 70g Potassium 2193mg

23. Crock Pot Mediterranean Pork

Preparation time: 10 minutes

Cooking time: 28 hours and 10 minutes

Servings: 6

INGREDIENTS:

- 3 pounds pork shoulder boneless
- For the marinade:
- ¼ cup extra virgin olive oil
- 2 teaspoons oregano
- ¼ cup lemon juice
- 2 teaspoons mustard
- 2 teaspoons mint
- 6 garlic cloves crushed
- 2 teaspoons pesto sauce
- Salt and black pepper to the taste

DIRECTIONS:

1. In a bowl, mix olive oil with lemon juice, oregano, mint, mustard, garlic, pesto, salt and pepper and stir very well.
2. Stab pork shoulder with a knife, rub it with the marinade, cover and keep in a cold place for 10 hours.
3. Flip pork shoulder and keep in a cold place for 10 more hours.
4. Transfer to your crock pot along with the marinade juices, cover and cook on low for 8 hours.
5. Uncover, transfer to platter and serve!
6. Enjoy!

NUTRITION: Calories 579, Fat 21.3g, Cholesterol 203mg, Sodium 436mg, Carbohydrate 20g, Fiber 3.7g, Sugars 9g, Protein 70.7g, Potassium 1160mg

24. Mediterranean Crock pot Orange Scented Roast

Preparation time: 10 minutes

Cooking time: 4 hours and 10 minutes

Servings: 8

INGREDIENTS:

- 1 pound new potatoes chopped
- 8 medium carrots cut in small pieces
- 15 ounces stewed tomatoes drained
- 1 yellow onion thinly sliced
- Zest and juice from 1 orange
- 4 garlic cloves thinly sliced
- 3 and ½ pounds pork roast trimmed
- 3 bay leaves
- Salt and black pepper to the taste
- ½ cup kalamata olives

DIRECTIONS:

1. Put potatoes in your crock pot.
2. Add carrots, tomatoes, onions, orange juice and zest.
3. Also add bay leaves, garlic and pork.
4. Season with salt and pepper, cover and cook on High for 4 hours.
5. Transfer meat to a cutting board, slice it and arrange it on a serving platter.
6. Discard bay leaves, add veggies to a bowl, crush the a little bit and mix with the olives
7. Add this mix to pork meat and serve!

8. Enjoy!

NUTRITION: Calories 579, Fat 21.3g, Cholesterol 203mg, Sodium 436mg, Carbohydrate 20g, Fiber 3.7g, Sugars 9g, Protein 70.7g, Potassium 1160mg

25. <u>Mediterranean Crock pot Pork Stew</u>

Preparation time: 20 minutes

Cooking time: 4 hours and 20 minutes

Servings: 4

INGREDIENTS:

- 2 pounds pork neck
- 1 tablespoon white flour
- 1 and ½ tablespoons extra virgin olive oil
- 2 eggplants chopped
- 1 brown onion thickly sliced
- 1 red capsicum cut in strips
- 3 garlic cloves finely chopped
- 1 tablespoon thyme
- 2 teaspoons sage leaves
- 14 ounces canned white beans drained
- 1 cup chicken stock
- 12 ounces zucchini thinly sliced
- 2 tablespoons tomato paste
- Bread rolls for serving

DIRECTIONS:

1. Put flour on a plate, add salt and pepper and mix.
2. Add pork, toss to coat, reserve flour and leave aside.
3. Heat up a pan with 2 teaspoons oil over medium high heat, add pork and cook for 3 minutes on each side.
4. Transfer pork to a crock pot and leave aside.

5. Heat up the rest of the oil in the same pan, add eggplant, onion, capsicum, thyme, sage and garlic, stir and cook for 5 minutes.
6. Add reserved flour, stir and cook for 1 more minute.
7. Transfer over pork, add beans, stock, tomato paste and zucchinis.
8. Cover and cook on High for 4 hours.
9. Uncover, transfer to plates and serve with bread rolls.
10. Enjoy!

NUTRITION: Calories 579, Fat 21.3g, Cholesterol 203mg, Sodium 436mg, Carbohydrate 20g, Fiber 3.7g, Sugars 9g, Protein 70.7g, Potassium 1160mg

26. Special Mediterranean Pork With Couscous

Preparation time: 10 minutes

Cooking time: 7 hours and 15 minutes

Servings:6

INGREDIENTS:

- 2 and ½ pounds pork loin boneless and trimmed
- ¾ cup chicken stock
- 2 tablespoons extra virgin olive oil
- ½ tablespoon paprika
- 2 and ¼ teaspoon sage
- ½ tablespoon garlic powder
- ¼ teaspoon rosemary
- ¼ teaspoon marjoram
- 1 teaspoon basil
- 1 teaspoon oregano
- Salt and black pepper to the taste
- 2 cups couscous cooked according to instructions

DIRECTIONS:

1. In a bowl, mix oil with stock, paprika, garlic powder, sage, rosemary, thyme, marjoram, oregano, salt and pepper to the taste and stir well.
2. Put pork loin in your crock pot, add stock and spice mix, cover and cook on Low for 7 hours.
3. Uncover, transfer pork to a cutting board, leave aside for a few minutes to cool down, cut, return to pot and stir gently with cooking juices.

4. Arrange pork loin on serving plates and serve with couscous on the side.
5. Enjoy!

NUTRITION: Calories 579, Fat 21.3g, Cholesterol 203mg, Sodium 436mg, Carbohydrate 20g, Fiber 3.7g, Sugars 9g, Protein 70.7g, Potassium 1160mg

SEAFOOD RECIPES

27. Luncheon Party Meal

Preparation Time: 20 minutes

Cooking Time: 4½ hours

Servings: 4

INGREDIENTS:

- 1 (14½-oz.) can diced tomatoes, drained
- 1 C. red sweet pepper, seeded and chopped
- 1 C. zucchini, sliced
- 2 garlic cloves, minced
- ½ C. dry white wine
- 8 oz. frozen medium shrimp, thawed
- 8 Kalamata olives, pitted and chopped roughly
- ¼ C. fresh basil, chopped
- 1 tbsp. olive oil
- 1½ tsp. fresh rosemary, chopped
- Salt, to taste
- 2 oz. feta cheese, crumbled

DIRECTIONS:

1. In a lightly greased crock pot, place the tomatoes, sweet pepper, zucchini, garlic and wine and mix well.
2. Set the crock pot on "Low" and cook, covered for about 4 hours.
3. Uncover the crock pot and stir in the shrimp.

4. Set the crock pot on "High" and cook, covered for about 30 minutes.
5. Uncover the crock pot and stir in the remaining ingredients.
6. Serve hot with the topping of feta cheese.

NUTRITION: Calories per serving: 206; Carbohydrates: 10.8g; Protein: 16.7g; Fat: 8.9g; Sugar: 5.5g; Sodium: 423mg; Fiber: 2.5g

28. Easiest Shrimp Scampi

Preparation Time: 15 minutes

Cooking Time: 1½ hours

Servings: 4

INGREDIENTS:

- 1 lb. raw shrimp, peeled and deveined
- ¼ C. chicken broth
- 2 tbsp. butter
- 2 tbsp. olive oil
- 1 tbsp. fresh lemon juice
- 1 tbsp. garlic, minced
- 1 tbsp. dried parsley
- Salt and freshly ground black pepper, to taste

DIRECTIONS:

1. In a crock pot, place all the ingredients and stir to combine.
2. Set the crock pot on "High" and cook, covered for about 1½ hours.
3. Uncover the crock pot and stir the mixture.
4. Serve hot.

NUTRITION: Calories per serving: 252; Carbohydrates: 2.6g; Protein: 26.4g; Fat: 14.8g; Sugar: 0.2g; Sodium: 406mg; Fiber: 0.1g

29. Amazingly Tasty Shrimp Orzo

Preparation Time: 15 minutes

Cooking Time: 3 hours 16 minutes

Servings: 6

INGREDIENTS:

- 2 C. uncooked orzo pasta
- 2 tsp. dried basil
- 3 tbsp. olive oil, divided
- 2 tbsp. butter
- 1½ tbsp. shallot, chopped
- 1 (14½-oz.) can diced tomatoes, drained
- 3 garlic cloves, minced
- 2 tsp. dried oregano
- 1 lb. jumbo shrimp, peeled and deveined
- 1 C. oil-packed sun-dried tomatoes, chopped
- 1½ C. Greek olives, pitted
- 2½ C. feta cheese, crumbled

DIRECTIONS:

1. In a large pan of the salted boiling water, cook the orzo for about 8-10 minutes or according to the package's directions.
2. Drain the orzo and rinse under cold running water.
3. Transfer the orzo into a large bowl with basil and 1 tbsp. of oil and toss to coat well. Set aside.
4. In a large skillet, heat the remaining oil and butter over medium heat and sauté the shallot for about 2-3 minutes.

5. Add the tomatoes, garlic and oregano and cook for about 1-2 minutes.
6. Add the shrimp and sun-dried tomatoes and cook for about 1 minute.
7. Remove from the heat and place the shrimp mixture into a greased crock pot.
8. Add the orzo mixture, olives and cheese and stir to combine.
9. Set the crock pot on "Low" and cook, covered for about 2-3 hours.
10. Serve hot.

NUTRITION: Calories per serving: 633; Carbohydrates: 57.9g; Protein: 35.4g; Fat: 30.2g; Sugar: 8.5g; Sodium: 1390mg; Fiber: 5.3g

30. Delightful Shrimp Pasta

Preparation Time: 15 minutes

Cooking Time: 7¼ hours

Servings: 4

INGREDIENTS:

- 1 (14½-oz.) can peeled tomatoes, chopped
- 1 (6-oz.) can tomato paste
- 2 tbsp. fresh parsley, minced
- 1 garlic clove, minced
- 1 tsp. dried oregano
- 1 tsp. dried basil
- 1 tsp. seasoned salt
- 1 lb. cooked shrimp
- Salt and freshly ground black pepper, to taste
- ¼ C. parmesan cheese, shredded

DIRECTIONS:

1. In a crock pot, place all the ingredients except for shrimp and Parmesan and stir to combine.
2. Set the crock pot on "Low" and cook, covered for about 6-7 hours.
3. Uncover the crock pot and stir in the cooked shrimp.
4. Sprinkle with parmesan cheese.
5. Set the crock pot on "High" and cook, covered for about 15 minutes.
6. Serve hot.

NUTRITION INFORMATION: Calories per serving: 212; Carbohydrates: 14.6g; Protein: 30.6g; Fat: 3.8g; Sugar: 7.9g; Sodium: 828mg; Fiber: 3.2g

31. Meltingly Tender Octopus

Preparation Time: 20 minutes

Cooking Time: 6 hours

Servings: 4

INGREDIENTS:

- 1½ lb. octopus
- 6 fingerlings potatoes
- ½ lemon, cut into slices
- Salt and freshly ground black pepper, to taste
- Water, as required
- 3 tbsp. extra-virgin olive oil
- 3 tbsp. capers

DIRECTIONS:

1. Remove the beak, eyes and any other parts of octopus.
2. Rinse the inside and outside of the octopus head and tentacles.
3. Cut off the head of the octopus at its base.
4. In a pan of the boiling water, dip the octopus with a pair of for about 10-15 seconds.
5. Now, place the octopus in a crock pot.
6. Place the potatoes, lemon slices, salt, black pepper and enough water to cover.
7. Set the crock pot on "High" and cook, covered for about 5-6 hours.
8. Uncover the crock pot and drain the octopus in a colander.

9. With a slotted spoon, transfer the potatoes onto a platter.
10. With paper towels, pat dry the potatoes and cut into thin slices.
11. Cut the octopus into thin slices.
12. In a large bowl, add the octopus, potatoes, oil, capers, salt and black pepper and toss to coat.
13. Serve immediately.

NUTRITION: Calories per serving: 308; Carbohydrates: 18.5g; Protein: 30.6g; Fat: 12.3g; Sugar: 1.6g; Sodium: 230mg; Fiber: 3.3g

32. Speedy Tilapia with Red Onion and Avocado

Preparation Time: 10 minutes

Cooking Time: 5 hours

Servings: 4

INGREDIENTS:

- 1 tablespoon extra-virgin olive oil
- 1 tablespoon freshly squeezed orange juice
- ¼ teaspoon kosher or sea salt
- 4 (4-ounce) tilapia fillets, more oblong than square, skin-on or skinned
- ¼ cup chopped red onion (about ⅛ onion)
- 1 avocado, pitted, skinned, and sliced

DIRECTIONS:

1. In a 9-inch glass pie dish, use a fork to mix together the oil, orange juice, and salt. Working with one fillet at a time, place each in the pie dish and turn to coat on all sides. Arrange the fillets in a wagon-wheel formation, so that one end of each fillet is in the center of the dish and the other end is temporarily draped over the edge of the dish. Top each fillet with 1 tablespoon of onion, then fold the end of the fillet that's hanging over the edge in half over the onion. When finished, you should have 4 folded-over fillets with the fold against the outer edge of the dish and the ends all in the center.

2. Cover the dish with plastic wrap, leaving a small part open at the edge to vent the steam. Microwave on high

for about 3 minutes. The fish is done when it just begins to separate into flakes (chunks) when pressed gently with a fork.

3. Top the fillets with the avocado and serve.

4. Prep tip: Because most fish skin is relatively thin, it cooks at about the same rate as fish flesh, which is why you can use this microwave method for both skin-on and skinless fish.

NUTRITION: Calories: 200; Total Fat: 11g; Saturated Fat: 2g; Cholesterol: 55mg; Sodium: 161 mg; Total Carbohydrates: 4g; Fiber: 3g; Protein: 22g

33. Grilled Fish on Lemons

Preparation Time: 10 minutes

Cooking Time: 10 hours

Servings: 4

INGREDIENTS:

- 4 (4-ounce) fish fillets, such as tilapia, salmon, catfish, cod, or your favorite fish
- Nonstick cooking spray
- 3 to 4 medium lemons
- 1 tablespoon extra-virgin olive oil
- ¼ teaspoon freshly ground black pepper
- ¼ teaspoon kosher or sea salt

DIRECTIONS:

1. Using paper towels, pat the fillets dry and let stand at room temperature for 10 minutes. Meanwhile, coat the cold cooking grate of the grill with nonstick cooking spray, and preheat the grill to 400°F, or medium-high heat. Or preheat a grill pan over medium-high heat on the stove top.

2. Cut one lemon in half and set half aside. Slice the remaining half of that lemon and the remaining lemons into ¼-inch-thick slices. (You should have about 12 to 16 lemon slices.) Into a small bowl, squeeze 1 tablespoon of juice out of the reserved lemon half.

3. Add the oil to the bowl with the lemon juice, and mix well. Brush both sides of the fish with the oil mixture, and sprinkle evenly with pepper and salt.

4. Carefully place the lemon slices on the grill (or the grill pan), arranging 3 to 4 slices together in the shape of a fish fillet, and repeat with the remaining slices. Place the fish fillets directly on top of the lemon slices, and grill with the lid closed. (If you're grilling on the stove top, cover with a large pot lid or aluminum foil.) Turn the fish halfway through the cooking time only if the fillets are more than half an inch thick. (See tip for cooking time.) The fish is done and ready to serve when it just begins to separate into flakes (chunks) when pressed gently with a fork.

5. Ingredient tip: We use the 10-minute-per-inch rule for grilling, baking, broiling, or panfrying any type of fish, since fish fillet sizes vary so much. Measure the thickest part of your fish fillets to determine the cooking time, and check the fish a minute or two before the suggested cooking time is up to prevent dried-out or overcooked fish. The fish is done when it just begins to separate into flakes (chunks) when pressed gently with a fork. The safe internal temperature for fish and seafood is 145°F.

NUTRITION: Calories: 147; Total Fat: 5g; Saturated Fat: 1g; Cholesterol: 55mg; Sodium: 158mg; Total Carbohydrates: 4g; Fiber: 1g; Protein: 22g

34. Weeknight Sheet Pan Fish Dinner

Preparation Time: 10minutes

Cooking Time: 10 hours

Servings: 4

INGREDIENTS:

- Nonstick cooking spray
- 2 tablespoons extra-virgin olive oil
- 1 tablespoon balsamic vinegar
- 4 (4-ounce) fish fillets, such as cod or tilapia (½ inch thick)
- 2½ cups green beans (about 12 ounces)
- 1 pint cherry or grape tomatoes (about 2 cups)

DIRECTIONS:

1. Preheat the oven to 400°F. Coat two large, rimmed baking sheets with nonstick cooking spray.
2. In a small bowl, whisk together the oil and vinegar. Set aside.
3. Place two pieces of fish on each baking sheet.
4. In a large bowl, combine the beans and tomatoes. Pour in the oil and vinegar, and toss gently to coat. Pour half of the green bean mixture over the fish on one baking sheet, and the remaining half over the fish on the other. Turn the fish over, and rub it in the oil mixture to coat. Spread the vegetables evenly on the baking sheets so hot air can circulate around them.
5. Bake for 5 to 8 minutes, until the fish is just opaque and not translucent. The fish is done and ready to serve

when it just begins to separate into flakes (chunks) when pressed gently with a fork.

6. Prep tip: To ensure that the fish cooks evenly, fold under any thin sections of the fillets so the entire fillet is half an inch thick.

NUTRITION: Calories: 193; Total Fat: 8g; Saturated Fat: 2g; Cholesterol: 55mg; Sodium: 49mg; Total Carbohydrates: 8g; Fiber: 3g; Protein: 23g

35. Crispy Polenta Fish Sticks

Preparation Time: 15 Minutes

Cooking Time: 10 hours

Servings: 4

INGREDIENTS:

- 2 large eggs, lightly beaten 1 tablespoon 2% milk
- 1 pound skinned fish fillets (cod, tilapia, or other white fish) about ½ inch thick, sliced into 20 (1-inch-wide) strips
- ½ cup yellow cornmeal
- ½ cup whole-wheat panko bread crumbs or whole-wheat bread crumbs
- ¼ teaspoon smoked paprika
- ¼ teaspoon kosher or sea salt
- ¼ teaspoon freshly ground black pepper
- Nonstick cooking spray

DIRECTIONS:

1. Place a large, rimmed baking sheet in the oven. Preheat the oven to 400°F with the pan inside.
2. In a large bowl, mix the eggs and milk. Using a fork, add the fish strips to the egg mixture and stir gently to coat.
3. Put the cornmeal, bread crumbs, smoked paprika, salt, and pepper in a quart-size zip-top plastic bag. Using a fork or tongs, transfer the fish to the bag, letting the excess egg wash drip off into the bowl before

transferring. Seal the bag and shake gently to completely coat each fish stick.

4. With oven mitts, carefully remove the hot baking sheet from the oven and spray it with nonstick cooking spray. Using a fork or tongs, remove the fish sticks from the bag and arrange them on the hot baking sheet, with space between them so the hot air can circulate and crisp them up.

5. Bake for 5 to 8 minutes, until gentle pressure with a fork causes the fish to flake, and serve.

6. Prep tip: The hands-free technique we use above to batter the fish is no-mess and works well for smaller fish sticks or chicken nuggets. Using a fork and coating the fish inside a bag keeps your fingers from getting messy and covered with batter.

NUTRITION: Calories: 256; Total Fat: 6g; Saturated Fat: 1g; Cholesterol: 148mg; Sodium: 321mg; Total Carbohydrates: 22g; Fiber: 2g; Protein: 29g

36. Salmon Skillet Supper

Preparation Time: 5 minutes

Cooking Time: 15 minutes

Servings: 4

INGREDIENTS:

- 1 tablespoon extra-virgin olive oil
- 2 garlic cloves, minced (about 1 teaspoon)
- 1 teaspoon smoked paprika
- 1 pint grape or cherry tomatoes, quartered (about 1½ cups)
- 1 (12-ounce) jar roasted red peppers, drained and chopped
- 1 tablespoon water
- ¼ teaspoon freshly ground black pepper
- ¼ teaspoon kosher or sea salt
- 1 pound salmon fillets, skin removed, cut into 8 pieces
- 1 tablespoon freshly squeezed lemon juice (from ½ medium lemon)

DIRECTIONS:

1. In a large skillet over medium heat, heat the oil. Add the garlic and smoked paprika and cook for 1 minute, stirring often. Add the tomatoes, roasted peppers, water, black pepper, and salt. Turn up the heat to medium-high, bring to a simmer, and cook for 3 minutes, stirring occasionally and smashing the tomatoes with a wooden spoon toward the end of the cooking time.

2. Add the salmon to the skillet, and spoon some of the sauce over the top. Cover and cook for 10 to 12 minutes, or until the salmon is cooked through (145°F using a meat thermometer) and just starts to flake.
3. Remove the skillet from the heat, and drizzle lemon juice over the top of the fish. Stir the sauce, then break up the salmon into chunks with a fork. You can serve it straight from the skillet.
4. Prep tip: There's a lot of confusion about wild vs. farm-raised fish, but the bottom line is that both fishing practices can be sustainable. These days, both wild and farmed fish are often harvested responsibly, meaning they have a minimal impact on the environment. To keep up to date on the best sustainable seafood choices on the market today, visit FishWatch.gov.

NUTRITION: Calories: 289; Total Fat: 13g; Saturated Fat: 2g; Cholesterol: 68mg; Sodium: 393mg; Total Carbohydrates: 10g; Fiber: 2g; Protein: 31g

VEGETABLES RECIPES

37. Quinoa and Tomatillos Casserole

Preparation time: 10 minutes

Cooking time: 4 hours

Servings: 4

INGREDIENTS:

- 1 cup low-fat Swiss cheese, shredded
- 12 ounces tomatillos, chopped
- 1 red bell pepper, chopped
- 1 pint cherry tomatoes, chopped
- ½ cup white onion, chopped
- 2 tablespoon oregano, chopped
- A pinch of black pepper
- 1 cup quinoa
- 1 tablespoon lime juice
- 2 pounds yellow summer squash, cubed
- Cooking spray

DIRECTIONS:

1. In a bowl, mix the tomatoes with tomatillos, onion, lime juice and black pepper and toss.
2. Grease your crock pot with the cooking spray and add quinoa.
3. Add half of the cheese and the squash and spread.
4. Add the rest of the cheese and the tomatillo mix, spread, cover and cook on Low for 4 hours.

5. Divide between plates, sprinkle oregano on top and serve.

NUTRITION: Calories 388, Fat 11.1g, Cholesterol 25mg, Sodium 203mg, Carbohydrate 50.1g, Fiber 10.1g, Sugars 8.3g, Protein 21.1g, Potassium 800mg.

38. Ginger Carrot Curry

Preparation time: 10 minutes

Cooking time: 4 hours Servings: 6

INGREDIENTS:

- 2 garlic cloves, minced
- 1 sweet potato, chopped
- 2 cups green beans, halved
- 1 tablespoon ginger, grated
- 1 teaspoon turmeric powder
- 2 teaspoons tamari sauce
- 1 carrot, chopped
- 1 small yellow onion, chopped
- 15 ounces canned chickpeas, drained and rinsed
- 28 ounces canned tomatoes, chopped
- 28 ounces coconut milk
- ¼ cup quinoa
- 1 and ½ cups water
- 1 teaspoon chili flakes

DIRECTIONS:

1. In your crock pot, combine the potato with green beans, carrot, onion, chickpeas, tomatoes, coconut milk, quinoa, garlic, ginger, turmeric, tamari, water and chili flakes, toss, cover and cook on Low for 4 hours.
2. Divide into bowls and serve.

NUTRITION: Calories 657, Fat 36.7g, Cholesterol 0mg, Sodium 173mg, Carbohydrate 70.1g, Fiber 19.9g, Sugars 18.3g, Protein 20.5g, Potassium 1565mg.

39. Hot Paprika Green Beans Mix

Preparation time: 10 minutes

Cooking time: 1 hour Servings: 4

INGREDIENTS:

- 2 pounds shrimp, peeled and deveined
- ½ pound green beans, trimmed and halved
- 1 tablespoon avocado oil
- ½ cup low-sodium veggie stock
- 1 tablespoon tomato juice
- ½ cup red onion, chopped
- 1 teaspoon hot paprika
- 2 tablespoons cilantro, chopped

DIRECTIONS:

1. In the crock pot, combine the shrimp with the green beans, oil and the other ingredients, put the lid on and cook on High for 1 hour.
2. Divide into bowls and serve.

NUTRITION: Calories 301, Fat 4.4g, Cholesterol 478mg, Sodium 604mg, Carbohydrate 9.6g, Fiber 2.4g, Sugars 1.7g, Protein 53g, Potassium 546mg

40. Cumin Black Bean Chili

Preparation time: 10 minutes

Cooking time: 4 hours

Servings: 4

INGREDIENTS:

- 2 garlic cloves, minced
- 1 teaspoon chipotle chili pepper, chopped
- 1 and ½ cups red bell pepper, chopped
- 1 tablespoon chili powder
- 1 cup yellow onion, chopped
- 1 and ½ cups mushrooms, sliced
- 1 tablespoon olive oil
- ½ teaspoon cumin, ground
- 1 cup tomatoes, chopped
- 16 ounces canned black beans, drained and rinsed
- 2 tablespoons cilantro, chopped

DIRECTIONS:

1. In your crock pot, combine the red bell peppers with onion, mushrooms, oil, chili powder, garlic, chili pepper, cumin, black beans and tomatoes, stir, cover and cook on High for 4 hours.
2. Divide into bowls, sprinkle cilantro on top and serve.

NUTRITION: Calories 469, Fat 5.9g, Cholesterol 0mg, Sodium 36mg, Carbohydrate 81.8g, Fiber 20g, Sugars 7.7g, Protein 27g, Potassium 2047mg.

41. **Classic Spinach and Artichoke Dip**

Preparation Time: 10 minutes

Cooking Time: 1 hour and 10 minutes

Servings: 2

INGREDIENTS:

- 11 Slices of Pita Bread, Sliced Into Rounds
- 1/3 Cup of Sun-Dried Tomatoes
- 1 Cup of Boiling Water
- 1 Can of Artichoke Hearts, Drained Quartered and Coarsely Chopped
- 1 Package of Spinach, Thawed, Drained and Air-Dried
- 1 Container of Soft Cream Cheese
- 1 Container of Sour Cream
- ¾ Cup of Fat-Free Milk
- ½ Cup of Feta Cheese
- ½ Cup of Onion, Diced
- ½ Cup of Mayo
- 1 Tbsp. of Vinegar, Specifically Red Wine Vinegar
- Dash of Salt and Pepper To Taste
- 2 Cloves of Garlic, Crushed

DIRECTIONS:

1. Preheat your over to 350 degrees.
2. Slice up your pita bread and with each slice and cut into small wedges. On a baking sheet place your beta bread into a single layer and bake for 10 minutes in your oven.

3. In a bowl combine both the sun-dried tomatoes and bowling water. Let this stand for at least an hour or until the tomatoes are soft.

4. Place your artichoke hearts and the last 11 ingredients into your crock pot and stir until thoroughly combined. Cover the pot with your lid and on the lowest setting cook the dip for 1 hour. Drain your sun-dried tomatoes and add into your crock pot.

5. Cook for an additional hour and serve dip with freshly toasted pita wedges and enjoy

NUTRITION: Calories 578, Fat 29.1g, Cholesterol 203mg, Sodium 210mg, Carbohydrate 6.5g, Fiber 2.1g, Sugars 2.7g, Protein 70.7g, Potassium 1142mg

42. Crispy Twice Baked Potatoes

Preparation Time: 15 minutes

Cooking Time: 8 hours and 26 minutes

Servings: 2

INGREDIENTS:

- 4 Small Potatoes
- Some Cooking Spray
- Dash of Salt and Pepper To Taste
- ¼ Cup of Milk
- ¼ Cup of Greek Yogurt
- 2 Ounces of Sharp Shredded Cheese
- 1 Tbsp. Of Fresh Chives, Finely Chopped
- 2 Slices of Bacon, Fully Cooked and Crumbled.

DIRECTIONS:

1. Scrub your potatoes and set aside to dry with paper towels. Coat each potato with a fine layer of cooking spray and pierce all over with a fork to ensure insides cook thoroughly. Sprinkle a little salt over each potato and place into your slow cook. Cover with lid and cook for 8 hours on the lowest temperature setting or until the potatoes are tender. Remove and allow to cool.

2. Once cooled cut each potato in half cutting lengthwise and scoop out the insides into a bowl that is microwave safe. Make sure that you leave the shells intact. In the bowl mash the pulp of the potatoes until smooth. Stir in your yogurt, milk, at least ½ cup of

shredded cheese, some salt and pepper until thoroughly mixed. Microwave your mixture for 1 minute on high or until it is thoroughly heated.

3. Spoon your mixture into each shell of potato until it fits evenly into each shell. Next sprinkle shredded cheese onto each potato or until fully coated. Place potatoes into your crock pot and cook on high for at least 25 minutes or until the cheese is fully melted. Once done remove from heat and sprinkle chives and bacon onto each potato. Serve as a side dish or a main course and enjoy.

NUTRITION: Calories 578, Fat 29.1g, Cholesterol 203mg, Sodium 210mg, Carbohydrate 6.5g, Fiber 2.1g, Sugars 2.7g, Protein 70.7g, Potassium 1142mg

43. Stuffed Red Bell Pepper

Preparation Time: 10 minutes

Preparation Time: 4 hours and 10 minutes

Servings: 3

INGREDIENTS:

- 2/4 Cup of Water
- ½ Cup of Couscous, Uncooked
- 2 Links of Italian Turkey Sausage
- Dash of Salt and Pepper
- ½ Cup of Garlic and Goat Herb Cheese, Divided and Crumbled
- 4 Small Red Bell Peppers
- 2 Tbsp. of Fresh Basil, Sliced

DIRECTIONS:

1. Bring your water to a nice rolling boil in a separate saucepan. Stir in your couscous gradually and remove the mixture from heat to let stand for five minutes. After five minutes, fluff with a fork.

2. While your couscous is left to stand cook your sausage in a non-stick skillet for four minutes or until browned on all sides over medium heat. Then stir in your couscous, salt, pepper and cheese.

3. As you stir prepare your red bell pepper and cut the tops off of it. Throw out the seeds and the membranes. On the inside of the peppers seasoning with a dash of salt and divide the remaining sausage mixture to use among all of the peppers.

4. Place the tops of the peppers back onto the peppers and place into your crock pot. Cover and cook on the lowest temperature setting for 4 hours or until the peppers are tender.
5. Remove the peppers and sprinkle the tops inside with cheese and fresh basil. Serve and enjoy.

NUTRITION: Calories 578, Fat 29.1g, Cholesterol 203mg, Sodium 210mg, Carbohydrate 6.5g, Fiber 2.1g, Sugars 2.7g, Protein 70.7g, Potassium 1142mg

44. Butter Green Peas

Preparation Time: 10 Minutes

Cooking Time: 3 Hours

Servings: 4

INGREDIENTS:

- 1 cup green peas
- 1 teaspoon minced garlic
- 1 tablespoon butter, softened
- ½ teaspoon cayenne pepper
- 1 tablespoon olive oil
- ¾ teaspoon salt
- 1 teaspoon paprika
- 1 teaspoon garam masala
- ½ cup chicken stock

DIRECTIONS:

1. In the crock pot, mix the peas with butter, garlic and the other ingredients,
2. Close the lid then cook it for 3 hours on High.

NUTRITION: Calories 121, Fat 6.5, Fiber 3, Carbs 3.4, Protein 0.6

45. Lemon Asparagus

Preparation Time: 8 Minutes

Cooking Time: 5 Hours

Servings: 2

INGREDIENTS:

- 8 oz asparagus
- ½ cup butter
- juice of 1 lemon
- Zest of 1 lemon, grated
- ½ teaspoon turmeric
- 1 teaspoon rosemary, dried

DIRECTIONS:

1. In your crock pot, mix the asparagus with butter, lemon juice and the other ingredients and close the lid.
2. Cook the vegetables on Low for 5 hours. Divide between plates and serve.

NUTRITION: Calories 139, Fat 4.6., Fiber 2.5, Carbs 3.3, Protein 3.5

46. Lime Green Beans

Preparation Time: 10 Minutes

Cooking Time: 2 Hours and 30 Minutes

Servings: 5

INGREDIENTS:

- 1-pound green beans, trimmed and halved
- 2 spring onions, chopped
- 2 tablespoons lime juice
- ½ teaspoon lime zest, grated
- 2 tablespoons olive oil
- ¼ teaspoon ground black pepper
- ¾ teaspoon salt
- ¾ cup of water

DIRECTIONS:

1. In the crock pot, mix the green beans with the spring onions and the other ingredients and close the lid.
2. Cook for 2.5 hours on High.

NUTRITION: Calories 67, Fat 5.6, Fiber 2, Carbs 4, Protein 2.1

DESSERT

47. Banana & Tortilla Snacks

Preparation Time: 5 minutes

Cooking Time: 0 minute

Servings: 1

INGREDIENTS

- flour tortilla (6 inches)
- tablespoons peanut butter
- 1 tablespoon honey
- 1 banana
- tablespoons raisins

DIRECTIONS

1. Lay the tortilla flat. Spread peanut butter and honey on the tortilla. Place the banana in the middle and sprinkle the raisins. Wrap and serve.

NUTRITION: 520 calories 19.3g fat 12.8g protein

48. Caramel Popcorn

Preparation Time: 30 minutes

Cooking Time: 1 hour

Servings: 20

INGREDIENTS

- 2 cups brown sugar
- 1/2 cup of corn syrup
- 1/2 teaspoon baking powder
- teaspoon vanilla extract
- 5 cups of popcorn

DIRECTION

2. Preheat the oven to 95° C (250° F). Put the popcorn in a large bowl.
3. Melt 1 cup of butter in a medium-sized pan over medium heat. Stir in brown sugar, 1 tsp. of salt, and corn syrup. Bring to a boil, constantly stirring — Cook without stirring for 4 minutes. Then remove from heat and stir in the soda and vanilla. Pour in a thin layer on the popcorn and stir well.
4. Place in two large shallow baking tins and bake in the preheated oven, stirring every 15 minutes for an hour. Remove from the oven and let cool completely before breaking into pieces.

NUTRITION: 14g fat 253 calories 32.8g carbohydrates

49. Apple and Berries Ambrosia

Preparation Time: 15 minutes

Cooking Time: 0 minutes

Serves 4

INGREDIENTS:

- 2 cups unsweetened coconut milk, chilled
- 2 tablespoons raw honey
- 1 apple, peeled, cored, and chopped
- 2 cups fresh raspberries
- 2 cups fresh blueberries

DIRECTION

1. Spoon the chilled milk in a large bowl, then mix in the honey. Stir to mix well.
2. Then mix in the remaining ingredients. Stir to coat the fruits well and serve immediately.

NUTRITION: 386 calories 21.1g fat 4.2g protein

50. Chocolate, Almond, and Cherry Clusters

Preparation Time: 15 minutes

Cooking Time: 3 minutes

Serving: 5

INGREDIENTS:

- 1 cup dark chocolate (60% cocoa or higher), chopped
- 1 tablespoon coconut oil
- ½ cup dried cherries
- 1 cup roasted salted almonds

DIRECTION

1. Line a baking sheet with parchment paper.
2. Melt the chocolate and coconut oil in a saucepan for 3 minutes. Stir constantly.
3. Turn off the heat and mix in the cherries and almonds.
4. Drop the mixture on the baking sheet with a spoon. Place the sheet in the refrigerator and chill for at least 1 hour or until firm.
5. Serve chilled.

NUTRITION: 197 calories 13.2g fat 4.1g protein

51. Chocolate and Avocado Mousse

Preparation Time: 40 minutes

Cooking Time: 5 minutes

Serving: 5

INGREDIENTS:

- 8 ounces (227 g) dark chocolate (60% cocoa or higher), chopped
- ¼ cup unsweetened coconut milk
- 2 tablespoons coconut oil
- 2 ripe avocados, deseeded
- ¼ cup raw honey

DIRECTION:

1. Put the chocolate in a saucepan. Pour in the coconut milk and add the coconut oil.
2. Cook for 3 minutes or until the chocolate and coconut oil melt. Stir constantly.
3. Put the avocado in a food processor, then drizzle with honey and melted chocolate. Pulse to combine until smooth.
4. Pour the mixture in a serving bowl, then sprinkle with salt. Refrigerate to chill for 30 minutes and serve.

NUTRITION: 654 calories 46.8g fat 7.2g protein

52. Coconut Blueberries with Brown Rice

Preparation Time: 55 minutes

Cooking Time: 10 minutes

Serving: 4

INGREDIENTS:

- 1 cup fresh blueberries
- 2 cups unsweetened coconut milk
- 1 teaspoon ground ginger
- ¼ cup maple syrup
- 2 cups cooked brown rice

DIRECTION

1. Put all the ingredients, except for the brown rice, in a pot. Stir to combine well.
2. Cook over medium-high heat for 7 minutes or until the blueberries are tender.
3. Pour in the brown rice and cook for 3 more minute or until the rice is soft. Stir constantly.
4. Serve immediately.

NUTRITION: 470 calories 24.8g fat 6.2g protein

53. **Glazed Pears with Hazelnuts**

Preparation Time: 10 minutes

Cooking Time: 20 minutes

Serving: 4

INGREDIENTS:

- 4 pears, peeled, cored, and quartered lengthwise
- 1 cup apple juice
- 1 tablespoon grated fresh ginger
- ½ cup pure maple syrup
- ¼ cup chopped hazelnuts

DIRECTION

1. Put the pears in a pot, then pour in the apple juice. Bring to a boil over medium-high heat, then reduce the heat to medium-low. Stir constantly.
2. Cover and simmer for an additional 15 minutes or until the pears are tender.
3. Meanwhile, combine the ginger and maple syrup in a saucepan. Bring to a boil over medium-high heat. Stir frequently. Turn off the heat and transfer the syrup to a small bowl and let sit until ready to use.
4. Transfer the pears in a large serving bowl with a slotted spoon, then top the pears with syrup.
5. Spread the hazelnuts over the pears and serve immediately.

NUTRITION: 287 calories 3.1g fat 2.2g protein

54. Keto Coconut Hot Chocolate

Preparation time: 15 minutes

Cooking time: 4 hours

Servings: 8

INGREDIENTS:

- 5 cups full-fat coconut milk
- 2 cups heavy cream
- 1 tsp vanilla extract
- 1/3 cup cocoa powder
- 3 ounces dark chocolate, roughly chopped
- ½ tsp cinnamon
- Few drops of stevia to taste

DIRECTIONS:

1. Add the coconut milk, cream, vanilla extract, cocoa powder, chocolate, cinnamon, and stevia to the crockpot and stir to combine.
2. Cook for 4 hours, high, whisking every 45 minutes.
3. Taste the hot chocolate and if you prefer more sweetness, add a few more drops of stevia.

NUTRITION: Calories: 135 Carbs: 5g Fat: 11g Protein: 5g

55. Ambrosia

Preparation time: 15 minutes

Cooking time: 3 hours

Servings: 10

INGREDIENTS:

- 1 cup unsweetened shredded coconut
- ¾ cup slivered almonds
- 3 ounces dark chocolate (high cocoa percentage), roughly chopped
- 1/3 cup pumpkin seeds
- 2 ounces salted butter
- 1 tsp cinnamon
- 2 cups heavy cream
- 2 cups full-fat Greek yogurt
- 1 cup fresh berries – strawberries and raspberries are best

DIRECTIONS:

1. Place the shredded coconut, slivered almonds, dark chocolate, pumpkin seeds, butter, and cinnamon into the crockpot.
2. Cook for 3 hours, high, stirring every 45 minutes to combine the chocolate and butter as it melts.
3. Remove the mixture from the crockpot, place in a bowl, and leave to cool.
4. In a large bowl, whip the cream until softly whipped.
5. Stir the yogurt through the cream.

6. Slice the strawberries into pieces, then put it to the cream mixture, along with the other berries you are using, fold through.
7. Sprinkle the cooled coconut mixture over the cream mixture.

NUTRITION: Calories: 57 Carbs: 11g Fat: 1g Protein: 1g

56. Dark Chocolate and Peppermint Pots

Preparation time: 15 minutes

Cooking time: 2 hours

Servings: 6

INGREDIENTS:

- 2 ½ cups heavy cream
- 3 ounces dark chocolate, melted in the microwave
- 4 egg yolks, lightly beaten with a fork
- Few drops of stevia
- Few drops of peppermint essence to taste

DIRECTIONS:

1. Mix the beaten egg yolks, cream, stevia, melted chocolate, and peppermint essence in a medium-sized bowl.
2. Prepare the pots by greasing 6 ramekins with butter.
3. Pour the chocolate mixture into the pots evenly.
4. Put the pots inside the crock pot and put hot water below halfway up.
5. Cook for 2 hours, high. Take the pots out of the crock pot and leave to cool and set.
6. Serve with a fresh mint leaf and whipped cream.

NUTRITION: Calories: 125 Carbs: 15g Fat: 6g Protein: 1g

CONCLUSION

The Mediterranean Diet is quickly gaining ground as the new best diet in the world. It's a healthy way of eating that focuses on vegetables, fruits, whole grains, beans, nuts and fish. And it does it all without breaking the bank!

In this book you'll find over 100 recipes for everything from soups to salads to main courses. The book is divided into 3 different sections: Breakfast, Main Dishes, and Side Dishes. Each section contains a variety of recipes that can be used as main dishes or side dishes.

There are lots of interesting and tasty recipes in this cookbook. Take a look through the book and see for yourself what you can make!

Looking for delicious, simple recipes for your crockpot? You're in the right place. Whether you want to pull dinner together quickly or need something easy to cook that everyone will love, we've got you covered.

The Mediterranean Diet Crock pot Cookbook collects the best of the best Mediterranean Diet recipes into one place, so you can enjoy a wide variety of delicious food with your family. Some of these recipes are indulgent and flavorful, while others are relatively low in fat and carbohydrates but big on flavor. Either way, they're guaranteed to please the entire family!

Our crock pot crock is one of the most popular kitchen appliances today, and there's a good reason why: It's a time-saver and it keeps your food hot or cold for hours without any additional work on your part. Plus, it makes cleanup so easy!

Cooking is an art form that we take very seriously here at Mediterranean Diet Crockpot Cookbook for Beginners. That's why we've included some of our best recipes in this book to help guide you through cooking real dishes--not just overpriced filler! We've also added some tips and advice from other cookbook authors to help you get started in the kitchen. No matter what you're looking for in a crock pot cookbook, we've got you covered with this collection of great recipes.

You've picked up the Mediterranean Diet Crockpot Cookbook for Beginners Crock-Pot Mediterranean Diet Crock pot Cookbook, your very own recipe book designed just for you! This cookbook contains over 250 recipes that are simple to make and easy to follow.

This cookbook caters to busy people on a budget. Every recipe takes Minutes to prepare and Ingredients you already have in your kitchen. Simple preparation and easy ingredients make these recipes perfect for cooking in the Mediterranean Diet Crockpot Cookbook for Beginners crock pot.

The Mediterranean Diet Crockpot Cookbook for Beginners Crock-Pot Mediterranean Diet Crock pot Cookbook gives you Recipes that will not only give you variety, but keep you and your family healthy. The recipes cover many different dietary needs, including: Italian, Indian, Greek, African, Meatloaf, and more!

For most people, it is difficult to constantly alter one's diet. In this book, every recipe can be customized by adding your favorite spices and fresh herbs to it before cooking it in your crock pot. For example: A recipe may call for a cup of chili peppers, while another calls for a full jar! Simply tweak the recipe and adapt it to your liking! The choices are up to you!

Ever forget that it's "dinner time"? With this book's variety of meals you can prepare them ahead of time like a meal from your favourite restaurant without skipping a step. Simply freeze them uncooked until you are ready to eat! You will not be disappointed!

CPSIA information can be obtained
at www.ICGtesting.com
Printed in the USA
BVHW062048010321
601387BV00008B/697

9 781801 655866